NAM

The Vietnam War

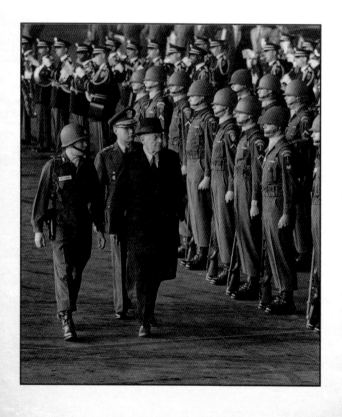

The International War

Published by Brown Bear Books Ltd

4877 N. Circulo Bujia
Tucson, AZ 85718
USA

and

First Floor
9-17 St. Albans Place
London N1 0NX

© 2013 Brown Bear Books Ltd

Reprinted in 2014

ISBN: 978-1-78121-046-8

Library of Congress Cataloging-in-Publication Data
available upon request

Editorial Director: Lindsey Lowe
Managing Editor: Tim Cooke
Design Manager: Keith Davis
Designer: Lynne Lennon
Picture Manager: Sophie Mortimer
Children's Publisher: Anne O'Daly
Production Director: Alastair Gourlay

Manufactured in the United States of America

CPSIA compliance information: Batch# AG/5550

Publisher's Note
Our editors have carefully reviewed the websites that appear
on page 47 to ensure that they are suitable for students. Many
websites change frequently, however, and we cannot guarantee
that a site's future contents will continue to meet our high
standards of quality. Be advised that students should be closely
supervised whenever they access the Internet.

Contents

INTRODUCTION

U p to the 1950s, Vietnam was a relative international backwater. For over a century, it had been part of the French colony of Indochina. But for more than a decade from the late 1950s to the mid–1970s, this small, undeveloped country became the focus of politics around the world.

Cold War flashpoint

The international flashpoint could have come in a number of countries. The fact that it came in Vietnam was largely a coincidence. In the aftermath of Vietnam's independence from France in 1954, the country split into a Communist North and a more democratic South. This development came at a tense period in the Cold War, the long stand-off between the United States and its allies on the one hand and the Communist Soviet Union and its allies on the other. Both sides tried to spread their international influence while avoiding direct military conflict.

U.S. politicians were determined to stop the spread of Communism. According to the so-called Domino Theory, the fall of even a relatively unimportant country like Vietnam to the Communists might result in its neighbors following suit. If that happened, the whole of Southeast Asia might fall under the influence of the Soviet Union or China.

Against the advice of the former French rulers, the United States government decided to take a stand. They would support South Vietnam, initially with economic assistance and military advice. When the Communists seemed to be gaining the upper hand, the United States committed air, ground, and naval forces. The original commitment grew to a peak in 1968, when some 536,000 U.S. personnel were serving in Vietnam.

International effort

The United Nations, the organization set up to settle international disputes, was opposed to the U.S. intervention. But the United States did not fight alone. A number of other countries from the Southeast Asia Treaty Organization (SEATO) also committed forces, including South Korea, Thailand, Australia, and New Zealand. On the Communist side, the Soviet Union and China supplied equipment and training to North Vietnam.

The most direct impact of the war was felt in Vietnam's immediate neighbors. The conflict spread to Cambodia and Laos, which were both politically destabilized. In Laos, the Communist Pathet Lao eventually seized power. In Cambodia, meanwhile, the country fell under the brutal Khmer Rouge, which murdered millions of citiizens.

Around the world, meanwhile, the conflict became a focus for protest. Students and many other groups in society took to the streets from the United States to Europe and Australia to protest what they saw as Western aggression.

◀ President John F. Kennedy addresses the United Nations General Assembly in September 1961.

◀ U.S. General William Westmoreland (center) and his Thai counterpart (right) welcome Thai troops to Vietnam.

Chapter 1

The Cold War

The Vietnam War was fought against the backdrop of the global struggle between the United States and Communist nations.

The Cold War was the name given to the hostility between the United States and its allies and the Communist countries of the world, led by the Soviet Union. The hostility lasted from the end of World War II in 1945 until the collapse of Communism in Europe between 1989 and 1992. The "war" was deadly earnest. Many Americans thought their freedoms and entire way of life were under threat if the Soviet Union was victorious. The war was "cold" rather than "hot" because there was almost no direct conflict between the two sides. Instead, there was mutual suspicion and hostility as both sides tried to influence other countries around the world. But there were flashpoints in which violence broke out in countries involved in the ideological struggle. When that happened, the superpowers took

▶ U.S. Secretary of State John Foster Dulles inspects U.S. troops in Berlin in 1959. Dulles was a leading "Cold Warrior."

▼ A huge nuclear missile is driven through Red Square in October 1964 as part of the annual parade of Soviet military might in Moscow.

sides and were happy to support their allies with financial and military support, as in Vietnam.

A spreading threat

The end of World War II left the Soviet Union in command of much of eastern Europe, which its military forces occupied after the ceasefire. The British prime minister Winston Churchill said that an "iron curtain" had fallen across Europe.

When Mao Zedong established a Communist government in China in 1949, it seemed to many in the West that the spread of Communism was gathering pace around the world. That same year, the United States and its allies founded the North Atlantic Treaty Organization (NATO), a military alliance that aimed to defend western Europe and North America against possible Communist aggression.

War in Korea

In 1950, the biggest military conflict in the years between World War II and the Vietnam War began in Korea. After World War II, Korea was divided along the 38th Parallel. North Korea became Communist, supported by the Soviet Union and China, while South Korea became a democracy backed by the United States and the United Nations.

When North Korean forces invaded South Korea in June 1950, U.S. forces led a UN coalition that fought both the North Koreans and their Chinese allies. The war ended in 1953. The border between North and South Korea remained in the same place.

The fear of Communism was widespread. The Soviet Union was a secretive and authoritarian society. Its government was not elected democratically and controlled

▼ Soviet leader Nikita Khrushchev examines items from the U.S. U-2 spy plane shot down in May 1960 in Soviet airspace.

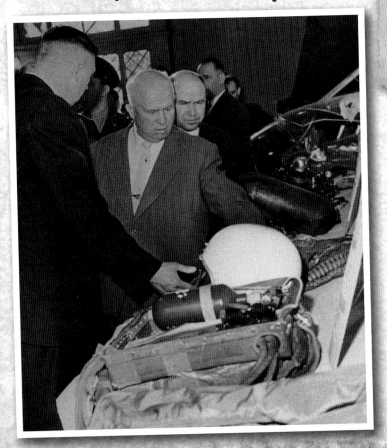

KEY MOMENT

Mao in China

Mao Zedong led a Communist revolution in China that in 1949 resulted in the creation of the People's Republic of China. Mao wanted to support Communism in other countries and saw a U.S. presence in Vietnam as a potential threat to China's border with Vietnam. He therefore agreed to North Vietnamese requests for support. The Chinese supplied Anti-Aircraft Artillery units as well as advanced weapons and other military hardware.

many aspects of Russians' daily lives. Communist belief (ideology) argued that Communism would eventually destroy capitalism and spread throughout the world. By the late 1950s it seemed that the Soviet Union was determined to challenge the international power of the United States and achieve a dominant world position.

Fighting and winning the Cold War became the principal aim of U.S. foreign policy. At times, some U.S. politicians became almost so obsessed with the threat posed by communism that they saw suspicious plots both abroad and at home where they probably did not exist. The Soviet Union in particular, however, did have an extensive network of secret agents who did spy for Moscow and certainly did plot against the United States.

Fighting the Cold War

The Cold War was contested directly and indirectly. Both the Soviet Union and the United States participated in some of the major flashpoints, committing their own troops, while in others the competing parties were allies of one or other superpower.

The countries of Africa, the Middle East, South Asia, and Southeast Asia emerged from World War II having to struggle to throw off rule by European colonial powers, most of whom were allied or friendly to the United States. These struggles were often armed, and the Soviet Union (and China) generally supported the rebels. During the 1960s, there were colonial struggles in Africa in French Algeria, Portuguese Africa, and British Aden and Rhodesia.

When they gained independence, the new nations were inherently unstable and weak. Both the United States and its allies and the Communist bloc became involved in the politics of these new nations and clashed as a result. Many leaders of the new nations looked with suspicion on the former colonial powers of the West, but were not attracted by Communism. In 1961, some countries formed the Nonaligned Movement, to try

▲ U.S. president John F. Kennedy and Soviet leader Nikita Khrushchev meet at a summit in Vienna, Austria, in June 1961.

to support one another without becoming dragged into the Cold War.

Growing crisis

In the early 1960s, the Cold War entered its most tense phase, triggered by three incidents. In May 1960 the Soviets shot down a U.S. U-2 spy plane hundreds of miles inside Soviet territory. The United States had

▲ President Johnson (right) looks on as Secretary of State Dean Rusk signs the nuclear Non-Proliferation Treaty with the Soviet Union in July 1968.

to admit to spying, and a scheduled meeting between President Dwight D. Eisenhower and the Soviet premier Nikita Khrushchev was cancelled.

When Eisenhower was replaced by the young and inexperienced John F. Kennedy, Khrushchev tried to intimidate the new U.S. president. Kennedy increased the military budget and strengthened U.S. forces. In August 1961, the Soviets began building the Berlin Wall, dividing West and East Germany. This was another potential flashpoint, but in reality the Soviets had built the wall to keep East Germans from fleeing to the West. In the third incident, U.S. intelligence discovered in October 1962 that the Soviet Union was

building missile bases in Cuba that would be able to strike at targets inside the United States. Kennedy ordered a build-up of U.S. military forces. While people around the world waited fearfully for the next move, Khrushchev backed down at the last moment. He agreed to remove the missiles in return for a U.S. promise not to invade Cuba.

The United States and the Soviet Union had come so close to war that it left both superpowers highly nervous. They agreed to set up a direct telex "hot line" between the White House and the Kremlin

▶ Chinese workers build an irrigation project in 1960. Under Mao, China supported the international spread of Communism.

to stop communication delays. In the late summer of 1963 they also agreed to ban all testing of nuclear weapons in the atmosphere or under the ocean.

Soviet leaders removed Khrushchev from power, partly because of the huge risk he had taken. But both sides expanded their military spending. Although the danger of nuclear conflict seemed to lessen, the arms race continued. Both sides looked for indirect ways to increase their influence in other parts of the world—and to block moves by the opposing side to do the same.

KEY PERSONALITY

Henry Kissinger

German-born Henry Kissinger became a leading expert on defense and international affairs as a professor at Harvard University. In 1969, Nixon appointed him as national security advisor. In 1973, Kissinger became secretary of state, a position he held until 1977. Kissinger saw himself as a practical man. He did not like the Communist influence in the world, but he was prepared to deal with the situation as it existed. He was the main U.S. policymaker in the peace talks with North Vietnam. He also led the process of détente, a relaxation of hostilities, with the Chinese and the Soviets.

Vietnam and the Cold War

The Vietnam War was the second phase of the Cold War in the 1960s. It was fought after the Vietnamese had overthrown their French colonial government in a long war that ended in 1954. In the aftermath of the conflict, the nationalist leader Ho Chi Minh established a Communist government in North Vietnam, with the backing of the Soviet Union and the Chinese. Fearing the fall of South Vietnam, the United States offered it, first, military advice and equipment and then increasing numbers of troops. The U.S. effort was supported by contributions from other countries that did not want to see Communism spread in Southeast Asia. One of the most significant contributions came from Australia, but there were also troops from regional powers that were geographically much closer to Vietnam, particularly South Korea and Thailand.

▼ **U.S. Navy personnel return home in 1969 after being held as prisoners in North Korea for nearly a year.**

Changing the Cold War

Involvement in the Vietnam War and the lack of a quick victory made many U.S. leaders and civilians less certain about how far it was possible to oppose the spread of Communism in that country. Not only were the sacrifices being made by young Americans greater than most people had feared; the war also did not seem to be turning the Vietnamese away from Communism. Supported by the Soviet Union and by the Chinese, the North Vietnamese and the Viet Cong in the South fought on determinedly, despite huge losses.

▲ President Nixon (right) greets Henry Kissinger in the White House in 1969.

The stalemate in Vietnam eventually contributed to the emergence of a new stage in the Cold War. This was known as détente, from a French word meaning "to relax." The United States and the Soviet Union began to back away from armed conflict. They opened talks aimed at reducing the number of nuclear weapons they both possessed. At about the same time, the United States also began official diplomatic contacts with Communist China.

By the 1980s the focus of the Cold War had moved to Afghanistan, which the Soviet Union invaded in 1979. This time, there was no U.S. military intervention—there would be no repeat of Vietnam.

KEY THEMES

The Nixon Doctrine

In August 1969, President Richard M. Nixon gave a speech in Guam. He set out what became known as the Nixon Doctrine. The president explained how he thought the United States should act in the future if faced with a situation like that in Vietnam. From now on, he said, the United States would be a friend and a protector to nations facing a Communist threat—but not a military protector. The United States would support its friends in other countries, but would expect them to do any fighting themselves. The Nixon Doctrine was intended to help develop a new, less tense, relationship with the Communist world.

Chapter 2

The Domino Theory

The roots of U.S. intervention in the civil war of a far-off country lay in a political view shaped by the tensions and anxieties of the Cold War.

At the start of the 1960s, most Americans had little idea of exactly where Vietnam was. But many Americans nevertheless believed that the United States should use its military power to help defend South Vietnam from the Communist North. Although the war would later become controversial and unpopular at home, when the first U.S. military advisors and special forces were sent to Vietnam in the late 1950s, there were few objections.

Eisenhower's explanation

One reason Americans were willing to become involved in fighting for a country more than 8,000 miles (12,900 km) away was the so-called domino theory. This was based on the belief that Communism could easily spread across borders between countries.

The name "domino theory" comes from what happens when a line of dominoes is set up standing close to one another and the first

▼ A French soldier watches out for Vietminh guerrillas during the French defeat at Dien Bien Phu in 1954.

▼ The French base at Dien Bien Phu was besieged for two months before the French surrendered.

is knocked over, beginning a chain reaction. President Dwight D. Eisenhower first used the analogy in a news conference in April 1954. "You have a row of dominoes set up, you knock over the first one, and what will happen to the last one is the certainty that it will go over very quickly. So you could have a beginning of a disintegration that would have the most profound influences."

Eisenhower was discussing the fate of Indochina—the present-day states of Vietnam, Laos, and Cambodia. At the time, the immediate crisis was the Communist-led resistance in Vietnam to French colonial rule. Eisenhower feared that if one country in the region came under Communist control then, one by one, they all would. A Communist Vietnam would put pressure on neighboring Thailand, Burma (Myanmar), and Malaya, and also on the newly independent—and huge—countries of Indonesia and India. In the worst-case scenario, not only would the whole of South and Southeast Asia become Communist. A row of dominoes falling in the region might also cause a row to fall in Africa or in Central America.

Eyes on Vietnam

The Americans' immediate concern when Eisenhower first discussed the domino theory was the French colony of Indochina. In 1946, after the end of World War II the previous year, France began military action against the Vietminh, Communist rebels led by Ho Chi Minh who wanted to set up an independent Vietnamese state.

KEY PERSONALITY

Dwight Eisenhower

Dwight D. Eisenhower became U.S. president in 1953. In World War II, he had served as Supreme Allied Commander in Europe. Eisenhower was concerned about the spread of Communism. Although he did not intervene in the war against French rule, he rejected the division of Vietnam and promised to support South Vietnam. He sent 900 U.S. military advisors to help combat Northern-backed uprisings. In 1960, Eisenhower warned incoming president John F. Kennedy that fighting Communism in Southeast Asia was a priority for the new U.S. government.

▲ John Foster Dulles, Eisenhower's secretary of state, supported an aggressive approach toward Communism.

In 1954, French forces were surrounded at a remote military base named Dien Bien Phu. Eisenhower discussed the situation with his Secretary of State, John Foster Dulles. Dulles told him "If Southeast Asia were lost, that would lead to the loss of Japan. The situation of Japan is hard enough with China being commie [communist]." It was becoming clear that, for the Eisenhower administration, the fate of Indochina itself was far less important than preventing the spread of Communism in the Pacific. The fact that the conflict was centered on Vietnam, as opposed to any other country, was little more than an accident. Yet although Eisenhower put U.S. bombers in the Philippines on standby to help the French, he did not send them in. He was reluctant to commit U.S. forces to battle again so soon after the end of the war in Korea, which had lasted from 1950 until 1953. After 55 days, the French at Dien Bien Phu surrendered, ending French rule in Indochina.

Although Eisenhower had not helped the French, in the longer term he made a commitment to use U.S. resources to fight the spread of Communism. In 1957

▶ President John F. Kennedy was warned by Eisenhower to make a priority of halting Communism in Southeast Asia.

KEY MOMENT

Korea Divided

The division of Vietnam in 1954 echoed what had happened in Korea at the end of World War II, when the victorious Allies divided it at the 38th Parallel. In 1948, Soviet-backed North Korea became a Communist state, while South Korea became a democratic republic. Tension grew until 1950, when North Korean forces invaded South Korea. Led by the United States, United Nations forces fought for South Korea. They pushed North Korean forces north, until the Chinese intervened on behalf of their Communist allies. The war ended in 1953 with the two countries again divided at the 38th Parallel.

he announced what became known as the Eisenhower Doctrine, which was to have profound influences for Vietnam. Eisenhower promised that the United States would come to the aid of any country threatened by Communism, whether by invasion or by civil war. The best way to avoid a chain of dominoes falling was to intervene when the first domino began to wobble.

U.S. involvement begins

At the 1954 peace conference in Geneva, Switzerland, France agreed to withdraw from Indochina. Cambodia and Laos would become independent. Vietnam would be divided along the 17th Parallel, creating a Communist North Vietnam and a noncommunist South Vietnam. All Vietnamese would be allowed to vote on the future of their country in national elections in 1956. Eisenhower agreed to send military advisors and military aid in order to support

▶ Zhou Enlai was China's premier from 1949 to 1976; he supported improved relations with the West.

KEY THEMES

Sukarno in Indonesia

One of the "dominoes" that concerned the United States was Indonesia. Since Indonesian independence in 1945, the country had been ruled by President Sukarno in a form of dictatorship known as "Guided Democracy." In the early 1960s Sukarno seemed to be steering Indonesia toward Communism. Backed by China and the Soviet Union, he took a stand against Western imperialism. In 1967, however, Sukarno was overthrown by General Suharto, whose anti-Communist policies made him a key ally of the West in the Cold War.

◄ Lyndon B. Johnson is sworn in as U.S. president after the assassination of John F. Kennedy in November 1963.

South Vietnam. That commitment did not change even when the South Vietnamese government refused to hold the elections specified in the peace agreement.

The South was concerned that Ho Chi Minh would win and take control of the whole country. Eisenhower agreed, even though this was undemocratic. In order to qualify for U.S. assistance under the Eisenhower Doctrine, a government did not have to be democratic: it simply had to be non-Communist.

Eisenhower's early support for South Vietnam was never intended to draw the United States into a war in Southeast Asia. The president was himself a highly senior former U.S. Army general who had commanded Allied forces in Europe in World War II. As early as 1951 he had noted in his diary a reason for not giving the French military aid in their war against the Vietminh:

KEY THEMES

Pathet Lao

The Pathet Lao grew out of the Laotian struggle against French rule in the 1950s. It was a Communist guerrilla organization led by Prince Souphanouvong with the backing of North Vietnam. During the Vietnam War, the Pathet Lao alternately formed weak coalitions with rightists and neutralists and fought against both them and the U.S. irregular forces operating in Laos. In 1975 the Laotian rightists and neutralists decided to allow the Pathet Lao to establish a government and abolish the Lao royal family.

KEY MOMENT

The Case of Thailand

Thailand, on the western border of Southeast Asia, had been a U.S. ally since 1948, and its military governments were never really threatened by a Communist takeover. Thailand had remained neutral during the war between the Vietnamese, whom it distrusted, and the French, who it saw as an imperialist power. But it backed the U.S. intervention in Vietnam and sent troops to fight. Thailand also became a major supply and transition point for U.S. forces, whose impact transformed the Thai economy, which became more modern and urban. Political power, however, remained in the hands of the military government.

"I am convinced no military victory is possible in that kind of theater."

Whatever Eisenhower's intention, however, both the specific commitments he made to South Vietnam and the general principle of the Eisenhower Doctrine ultimately led to the commitment of U.S. ground forces to the war in Vietnam in 1965.

Increasing involvement

The decision to commit regular U.S. Army troops and U.S. Marines to Vietnam was actually taken by President Lyndon B.

► Ho Chi Minh poses with child recruits from the North Vietnamese Army. Ho's communism made the United States highly suspicious of his intentions.

Johnson. But before Johnson, Eisenhower's sucessor, President John F. Kennedy, had also maintained the U.S. commitment to the domino theory. The early years of Kennedy's brief administration (he was assassinated after less than three years in office) were dominated by tension with the Soviet Union. When the Soviets built missile bases on Cuba in 1962, it seemed that the two superpowers were very close to nuclear war. Kennedy's reaction was to order a military buildup and to use U.S. Navy ships to stop and search vessels heading to Cuba. In such an atmosphere of hostility, Kennedy

▲ Vietnam was divided at the 17th Parallel; the two states were split by a 6-mile (10-km) demilitarized zone (DMZ).

maintained the commitment to supplying South Vietnam with military supplies and with advisors, usually either U.S. Marines or special forces such as Green Berets. These U.S. personnel were tasked with helping the Army of the Republic of Vietnam (ARVN) to fight the Communist North Vietnamese Army (NVA). They provided training and advice to ARVN troops. By the time Johnson became president in November 1963, the violence was growing and there had been U.S. casualties. With U.S. politicians still committed to the domino theory, Johnson took the decision to commit ground forces. The next stage of the global war against Communism would start on Vietnamese soil.

Chapter 3

International Involvement

The United States did not fight alone in Vietnam. A number of other countries also sent military personnel.

The Americans provided the largest number of non-Vietnamese combatants, but both North and South Vietnam were militarily supported by other powers. The support often took the form of financial aid or military hardware, but there were also numerous foreign troops in Vietnam. The distribution of those troops reflected regional concerns as well as the global situation of the Cold War. Most of the military contingents came from Southeast Asia or the Pacific region.

Backing for the North

North Vietnam was supported by both the leading Communist superpowers—the People's Republic of China and the Soviet Union. China had supported Ho Chi Minh's Vietminh since the Vietnamese war against the French in the 1950s. But China had been defeated when its forces fought with Communist North Korea in the Korean

▼ Australian troops land on a beach in South Vietnam.

War (1950–1953), and it remained nervous of provoking the United States. But China provided valuable material support to the Vietnamese communists. From 1965, China sent anti-aircraft units and engineering battalions to North Vietnam. Their contribution lasted until the Chinese withdrew from Vietnam in 1970.

Meanwhile, the Soviet Union supplied intelligence vessels in the South China Sea, which could warn North Vietnamese forces of long-range U.S. B-52 bombers flying from Okinawa and Guam. The Soviets also supplied hardware such as tanks, planes, helicopters, and artillery, together with medical supplies. More than 10,000 Vietnamese fighters were trained in the Soviet Union. At various times from 1965 to 1974, up to 3,000 Soviet troops were secretly stationed inside Vietnam, including anti-aircraft crews who shot down U.S. aircraft.

▲ Australians wait to be transported to their base after arriving in South Vietnam in 1965.

Other Northern allies

More hardware for North Vietnam came from North Korea. In early 1967, the North Korean government sent a squadron of fighter planes and pilots to help in the defense of Hanoi. However, they were only there for a year or two, together with two anti-aircraft artillery regiments. After the war, U.S. prisoners of war such as future senator and presidential candidate John McCain reported that they

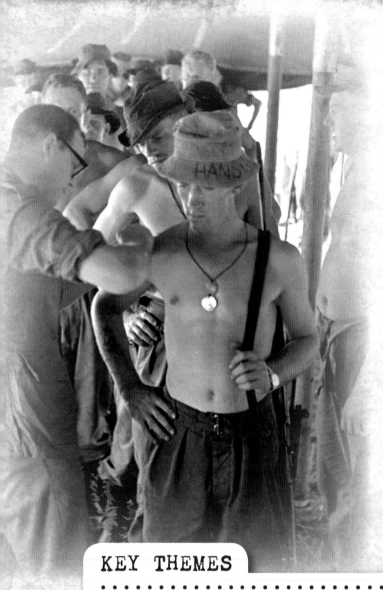

had encountered Cuban military personnel during their captivity in Vietnam. The full extent of any Cuban involvement, however, remains unknown.

Backing for the South

The forces fighting for South Vietnam were led by the United States. The second largest group came from South Korea. They started arriving in 1964 in response to a request from U.S. president Lyndon B. Johnson. The first combat battalions began arriving a year later, reaching a peak of 50,000 in 1968. Before they withdrew in 1973, a total of 320,000 South Korean troops served a one year tour of duty in Vietnam. Their effectiveness was acknowledged by their U.S. allies, who also paid the Korean soldiers, greatly boosting the

◀ Australian troops are inoculated against smallpox at the Bien Hoa Air Base in June 1965.

KEY THEMES

The Soviet Contribution

The Soviet Union sent few combat troops to support North Vietnam. Some estimates suggest that a force of perhaps 3,000 men served in the conflict. The Soviets were anxious to avoid escalating U.S. involvement in Vietnam. At the same time, however, they gave the Army of North Vietnam (NVA) excellent training. They also supplied the latest military hardware, including the AK-47 infantry rifle and ground-to-air missiles.

South Korean economy. The South Korean commitment in Vietnam was, however, marred by accusations of atrocities carried out against South Vietnamese civilians.

Australia and New Zealand

Both Australia and New Zealand sent ground soldiers to serve in Vietnam. The military commitment reflected the two countries' diplomatic commitment to the anti-Communist side in the Cold War. As Pacific powers, they shared the U.S. anxiety about the "domino theory," according to which a Communist victory in Vietnam would threaten the spread of Communism throughout Southeast Asia and Indonesia. That would leave Australasia isolated from the

KEY THEMES

Korean Forces

South Korean forces in Vietnam reached a peak of 48,000 in 1969. They included elite units such as the Capital (Tiger) Division, and operated mainly in Binh Dinh Province. The Koreans were renowned for their military effectiveness, but they were later accused of war crimes. The Koreans also fell out with their U.S. allies, who refused to finance Korea's military commitment in Vietnam.

◄ A member of the Australian Special Forces teaches a Vietnamese Ranger recruit how to fire a grenade launcher.

KEY THEMES

. . . .

"More Flags" Campaign

In 1967 President Lyndon Johnson began a "More Flags" campaign to get allies to support the U.S. war effort. Thailand, Australia, New Zealand, South Korea, and the Philippines all sent troops. The tiny island of Taiwan sent 31 men. Spain, led by the dictator General Franco, sent a 13-man medical team. Other countries sent medical supplies. The Swiss sent microscopes, while the British supplied a printing press.

"free world." They were also members of the Southeast Asian Treaty Organization (SEATO), set up by the United States to combat Communism.

About 60,000 Australians served in Vietnam throughout the whole war, peaking at about 7,500 men. They were supplemented by some 7,000 New Zealanders, most of whom were attached to the 1st Australian Task Force. The first 30 Australian advisors arrived in 1962, with ground forces arriving in 1964. To begin with, the Australasian forces were far more experienced in jungle warfare than their U.S. allies, and played an advisory role. In 1965, in order to increase the Australian military commitment, Prime Minister Robert Menzies introduced military conscription. The move was highly unpopular, both within the Australian Army and in the wider civilian population.

1st Australian Task Force

Based in Phuoc Tay province, the 1st Australian Task Force fought its own strategic war, independent of U.S. activities. There were also contributions from the Australian Air Force, which carried out bombing raids and provided close-air support,

◀ Members of the Thai "Black Panther" Division arrive in Vietnam in 1968.

and the Royal Australian Navy, whose destroyers bombarded enemy positions along the coast.

Australian forces had mixed fortunes in the fighting. At the Battle of Long Tan in August 1966, they decisively fought off an attack on their position by a Viet Cong regiment, despite being heavily outnumbered. The Australians lost 18 men, but the Viet Cong left behind 245 dead and was never again able to challenge Australian control of Phuoc Tay province. On the other hand, heavy losses in February 1968 convinced Australian commanders of the need to bring tanks to Vietnam to support the infantry. The Communist attacks of the Tet Offensive in January 1968, although unsuccessful, meanwhile undermined support for the war

KEY THEMES

Australian Forces

The Australian Army Training Team Vietnam (AATTV) served from 1962 until 1972. It was one of the longest serving units of the war. This elite group, which included Australians and New Zealanders, trained the South Vietnamese in jungle warfare. A larger Australian commitment began in 1966, with the formation of 1st Australian Task Force. It was militarily successful but caused bitter arguments at home.

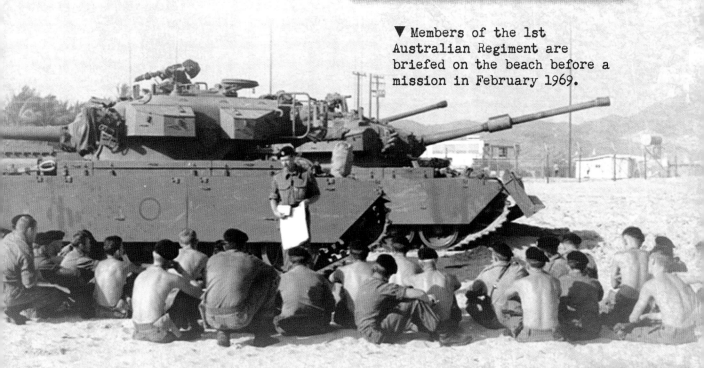

▼ Members of the 1st Australian Regiment are briefed on the beach before a mission in February 1969.

► This is the heavily guarded headquarters of South Korean forces in Saigon.

KEY THEMES

The Hmong

Among the allies of the United States were the Hmong of northern Laos, who saw both the North Vietnamese and the Pathet Lao as threats. More than 10,000 Hmong were recruited by the CIA to serve in irregular forces under General Vang Pao. They controlled the Plain of Jars in central Laos, and monitored the Ho Chi Minh Trail. Eventually, the Hmong were defeated. After reprisals by the Vietnamese and the Pathet Lao, the Hmong were nearly wiped out.

at home, just as they did in the United States. The Australians now decided not to increase their troop commitment to Vietnam, although forces remained on the ground, keeping control of Phuoc Tay province. Near the end of the war, the 1st Australian Task Force fought in the Battle of Binh Ba, clearing the village in fighting that left 107 Communists dead against just one Australian.

More support for the South

Among the other regional powers to send troops to South Vietman were the Philippines and Thailand, who were both strong allies of the United States. The 10,500 Filipino troops did not fight but took part in medical and other civic duties. The Thais, on the other hand, were deeply involved in the secret war in Laos between 1964 and 1972. Laos bordered Thailand, which was alarmed by the prospect of Communism spreading into its neighbor. Thai regular and irregular troops kept watch on Communist activity on the Ho Chi Minh Trail. They fought with the United States and South Vietnamese against the North Vietnamese and their Pathet Lao Communist guerrilla allies.

The government of the Republic of China had been based on the island of Taiwan since Mao Zedong's Communists had taken over China in 1949. They remained bitterly hostile toward mainland China, and were close allies of the United States. The United States did not recognize the Chinese Communist government until 1979. The Taiwanese did not provide fighting troops, but from November 1967, they secretly provided cargo transportation for U.S. forces and helped to train South Vietnamese troops in specialist skills such as diving.

▼ Members of the Republic of Korea Tiger Division patrol in the Central Highlands at the end of 1969.

Chapter 4

The World's Viewpoint

The war in Vietnam provoked strong reaction around the world. Many people saw the U.S. role as an echo of colonial conflicts.

The Vietnam War was more than just a regional conflict. It was one of the flashpoints of the global Cold War that had begun after the end of World War II in 1945. The United States and its allies were intent on limiting the global influence of the Soviet Union and its Communist allies. As the colonial world disintegrated in Asia and Africa, both superpowers supported their allies, as in the civil war that began between Communist North Korea and South Korea in 1950. The war that broke out between North and South Vietnam in 1954 drew global attention.

Southeast Asia

The countries most closely associated with the conflict were inevitably Vietnam's immediate neighbors—Laos and Cambodia—

▶ Demonstrators march in Dortmund, Germany, in the late 1960s. The banner reads "Stop the U.S. war. Peace in Vietnam, now!"

◀ Led by President De Gaulle, France was the only major U.S. ally to openly oppose the war in Vietnam.

The initial members of SEATO, along with the United States, Britain, and France, included Australia, New Zealand, Pakistan, the Philippines, and Thailand. Under pressure from the Communist government in China, Laos, Cambodia, and South Vietnam had only partial membership under a special protocol that allowed them to appeal for help from other members to fight aggression from an external power. However, SEATO had no military forces of its own. It had to depend on troops and hardware provided by its member states. The process for committing troops to action was so complex that it made it difficult to accomplish.

and the other nations of Southeast Asia, such as Thailand. Many of these countries were members of the Southeast Asia Treaty Organization (SEATO), which had been formed in 1955 as an eastern version of the North Atlantic Treaty Organization (NATO), founded by the United States and its allies the previous year. Both organizations were aimed at fighting the spread of Communism.

Shifting concerns

Since its formation, SEATO had been mainly concerned about fighting in Laos between the Communist Pathet Lao, neutralist forces, and rightists. The Pathet Lao was supported by North Vietnamese troops, and the Soviet Union and China also lent support. The United States sent 5,000 military personnel to northeast Thailand. But when a new government took over in Laos, both Laos and Cambodia withdrew from SEATO.

SEATO's focus shifted to Vietnam. But the French had no wish to become involved in its former colony. They believed that further military involvement in the region would end in disaster, and effectively pulled out of SEATO. Pakistan also played no part, and the British were also lukewarm about intervening in the Vietnam War.

The other members of SEATO, however—the United States, Australia, New Zealand, the Philippines, and Thailand—all offered

▲ The Soviet leader Leonid Brezhnev suggested that Soviet forces would become involved in Vietnam, but in fact few did so.

KEY THEMES

United Nations

The United Nations (UN) had been formed after World War II as an international security organization. In 1965, the UN condemned U.S. and other international involvement in Vietnam. For the United Nations to become involved either way, however, would have involved a vote in the Security Council. There, either the Soviet Union or the United States would have vetoed any proposed course of action seen as advantageous to the other's allies. Instead, the UN building in New York City became a focus for protest against the war.

military assistance to South Vietnam. They claimed that their SEATO commitments obliged them to help South Vietnam resist aggression. In fact, action in Vietnam was undertaken by each nation individually, not as part of any SEATO operation.

The U.S. withdraws

As the fighting against North Vietnam and the Viet Cong increasingly became deadlocked on the ground, the lack of political progress underlined the political weakness of SEATO. The United States decided that SEATO was not the best way to achieve its ends in Southeast Asia. In July 1969 U.S. president Richard Nixon declared the so-called Nixon Doctrine. Nixon said that the United States would not become involved in another war in Southeast Asia. That effectively ended its military commitment to SEATO. When Nixon visited Beijing in February 1972, that reduced the fear of Chinese influence spreading in the region. And after a coup overthrew Prince Sihanouk in Cambodia in March 1970, SEATO calls for a diplomatic solution that would remove North Vietnamese troops from Cambodia were simply ignored.

KEY THEMES

. . . .

Rise of terrorism

One phenomenon related to the Vietnam War was the growth of terrorism in Western countries. The Weathermen in the United States and groups such as the Red Army Faction in Europe used bombing and assassination to target the establishment. Among the objects of their protests were U.S. involvement in Vietnam, which they saw as colonialist.

◀ The United Nations Security Council in session in 1966. The UN was not able to influence events in Vietnam to any real degree.

▶ A German supermarket promotes U.S. food in 1967, as part of efforts to increase U.S. trade with Europe.

View from Europe

The major European powers meanwhile—France, Great Britain, and Germany—looked at the conflict in Vietnam from viewpoints that reflected their relevant experience. France was the country that had been most closely linked with the region in the past, governing the colony of Indochina—now Vietnam, Cambodia, and Laos—from 1887 until its military defeat in 1954.

After their own withdrawal from Southeast Asia, the French had warned the United States of the risks of becoming involved in the civil war in Vietnam, but their warnings had been ignored. The French president, General de Gaulle, believed that the United States had ambitions to replace French influence in the region, but that any military involvement was doomed to failure.

More importantly, De Gaulle believed that the threat from Communism was not as great as U.S. politicians feared. Eventually, the Frenchman thought that Communism was a form of rebellion that would only be temporary. Far more significant, in De Gaulle's eyes, was the role of nationalism in Vietnam. In order to restore stability in the country, De Gaulle believed the best way was to make an agreement with Communist China. But while the French recognized Chairman Mao's government in Beijing, the United States refused to do so until 1979.

Britain's response

In Britain, political support for the Vietnam War was also lukewarm. The British did not approve of the decision to cancel South Vietnamese elections in 1956, even though the cancellation was supported by the United States. In addition, the British still had important imperial possessions in South

◄ A symbol of "Peace through Understanding," the Unisphere was part of the New York World's Fair in 1964. But the Cold War world was far from unified.

KEY MOMENT

KEY MOMENT

Paris Riots

In May 1968 French students began a protest about visitors of the opposite sex to dorm rooms. French society was full of tenions, and the protest quickly became a full-scale occupation of the University of the Sorbonne, accompanied by violent confrontation with the authorities in Paris. More than 10 million workers, some 50 percent of all French workers, went on strike to support the protests. For several weeks, it seemed that the economy would entirely break down. The riots in France echoed the contemporary riots against the war in the United States, and U.S. aggression in Vietnam was one of the rallying points of the protests.

and East Asia, in Hong Kong, Singapore, and Malaya. Once conflict broke out in Vietnam, therefore, they preferred a negotiated settlement to end hostilities before they could escalate into a full-scale conflict that might draw in the whole region.

British politicians hoped that they would be able to influence the Americans to moderate their use of military power in Southeast Asia. But the British were also so eager to maintain their traditional "special relationship" with the United States that they dare not offend their potential allies. That mean that their pressure had no effect, despite the efforts of Prime Minister Harold Wilson. For their own

◀ Antiwar protestors in Paris, France, hang an effigy of President Lyndon Johnson in February 1968.

▲ In October 1968 about 100,000 people in London, Britain, marched against the Vietnam War.

part, the British steadfastly refused to make a military commitment in Vietnam, despite U.S. pressure and Britain's membership of SEATO.

Divisions in Germany

Germans, meanwhile, understood the situation in Vietnam as well as anyone. Since 1945, Germany had been divided between the free West and the Communist East. The West German chancellor Ludwig Erhard announced that there was no country closer to Vietnam than Germany, despite the physical and cultural distance between them.

The U.S. national Security Advisor, McGeorge Bundy, remarked that "The defense of Berlin, right now, is in Vietnam." But although the West German goverment enthusiastically supported the U.S. fight against Communism, they refused requests for military support or even for a military hospital. It did, however, send the S.S. *Helgoland* to serve as a hospital ship in Saigon from 1966 to 1972. In Cold War Germany, reinforcing the security of Germany itself was more important than fighting Communism in distant Vietnam.

Chapter 5

Postwar Asia

The Vietnam War continued to shape politics in Southeast Asia for years after the fighting ended.

The United States had entered the war in Vietnam because the Domino Theory version of foreign affairs suggested that allowing South Vietnam to be taken over by Communist North Vietnam would increase the threat of communism spreading throughout Southeast Asia. The defeat of the world's greatest superpower by an army of Communist rebels allowed exactly that to happen. Not only was the newly unified Vietnam Communist, but in neighboring Laos the Communist Pathet Lao took control. In Cambodia, meanwhile, the consequences resulted in national tragedy.

The pro-American general Lon Nol had seized power in Cambodia in 1970. His unpopularity encouraged support for the Communist Khmer Rouge guerrillas led by Pol Pot. In 1973 the Khmer almost captured

◀ The UN headquarters in New York was a focus of antiwar protest. In November 1965, a protestor burned himself to death in front of the building.

▲ This recruitment poster calls for volunteers for the Chinese navy. By the mid-1970s, however, China's relations with the rest of the world had improved greatly.

the capital, Phnom Penh. The capital was saved by U.S. bombing raids on the attackers, but the raids left the Cambodian economy in ruins. The popularity of the Khmer Rouge grew, and Pol Pot's Communist beliefs became more radical.

Cambodia's killing fields

By 1975, the United States had lost interest in the region. When Pol Pot again advanced on Phnom Penh, Lon Nol realized that defeat was inevitable and surrendered.

Pol Pot renamed the country the People's Democratic Republic of Kampuchea. Inspired by Marxist Communism, Pol Pot drove millions of Cambodians from the cities into the countryside. He wanted to re-create a pre-industrial, rural, peasant economy. Cambodians were forced to live on collective farms under strict rules. The Khmer Rouge murdered all those they accused of being "intellectuals." That included not just academics, but anyone who had trained for a professional or skilled job, such as engineers. Some people were executed as intellectuals for wearing spectacles. Nearly 30 percent of the Cambodian population were killed in what were named "the killing fields."

Vietnam in ruins

In Vietnam itself, the Communists had won the war, but the country they now controlled had suffered nearly 30 years of warfare. Its economy was barely functioning. Its

▶ Chinese sailors study "The Thoughts of Chairman Mao" in 1968. Mao's philosophy still dominated China in the post Vietnam War period.

Recovery of Saigon

After the fall of the South in 1973, Saigon was renamed Ho Chi Minh City. The city had suffered greatly during the years of fighting, but it remained the economic capital of Vietnam. Its economy had been boosted by the millions of dollars spent by U.S. military personnel during the war. A large hospitality sector had emerged, based on hotels, bars, restaurants, and other forms of entertainment. Although Hanoi far to the north remained the political capital, the real economic power still lay in the south. When Vietnam's government relaxed rules on economic enterprise in the 1980s, it was Ho Chi Minh City that reaped most of the benefits.

transportation system and cities lay in ruins. Millions of Vietnamese had been displaced and lived as refugees. The war had left more than a million widows, and more than 850,000 orphaned children.

Faced with a Communist government, as many as 1.5 million South Vietnamese and ethnic Chinese living in North Vietnam fled the country, many on leaky, overcrowded, and barely seaworthy boats and rafts. Their numbers rose after Vietnam again went to war, in 1978, this time against the Chinese.

These so-called "boat people" faced a struggle to reach safety. As many as 200,000 are estimated to have drowned, starved to death, or been killed by pirates; more ended up in overcrowded refugee camps in Hong Kong. But nearly a million also survived and went on to live in societies around the world.

▼ Japanese scientists work on a satellite program in 1966. Japanese technology made huge advances in the 1960s.

Meanwhile, Communist reprisals against their former enemies in South Vietnam included the execution of up to 60,000 "undesirables." Another million were sent to "reeducation" camps to be taught to believe in Communist ideology. An estimated 165,000 people died in the camps, but within a few years most of the survivors were beginning to rejoin Vietnamese society.

They found a country that was still one of the poorest in the world. It was also internationally isolated, because Chinese and U.S. relations had improved since the end of the war. Vietnam's only international aid came from the Soviet Union. Farmers struggled to produce enough food to feed the population, while inflation meant that workers' wages did not keep up with the general rise in prices.

KEY MOMENT

- -

Rise of Japan

The struggle between Communism and democracy that lay at the heart of the Cold War eventually ended with the collapse of the Soviet Union in 1991. By then, however, it had become clear that the best economic model for Asian nations was not the centralized Communist state the Americans had feared. Instead, many nations in Asia looked to Japan as an example of how to develop. Since World War II Japan had pursued a policy of specialization in high-tech electronic and automotive industries. Countries such as Vietnam, Korea, and even China eventually began to follow a similar economic strategy.

▲ Many Khmer Rouge soldiers were young, like this child photographed with his rocket-propelled grenade launcher.

Toward war in Cambodia

On the border with Cambodia, fighting between the Vietnamese and the Khmer Rouge continued after the end of the Vietnam War. Pol Pot was afraid that Vietnam would try to put itself in a leading role in a Southeast Asian federation. The Vietnamese, meanwhile, worried that Pol Pot's government would increase China's power in the region. In December 1978 the tension boiled over and 150,000 Vietnamese troops invaded Cambodia. They defeated Pol Pot within two weeks and established the new People's Republic of Kampuchea.

Internationally, the Vietnamese invasion of Cambodia was widely condemned. Vietnam was even more isolated than before. The Chinese who had backed Pol Pot invaded the northern provinces of Vietnam in February

KEY MOMENT

Vietnam–Cambodian War

The North Vietnamese and the Khmer Rouge of Cambodia had been allies against the United States during the Vietnam War, but after the war the Khmers became suspicious that the Vietnamese would try to dominate the whole of Southeast Asia. They began to expel or execute Vietnamese-trained personnel. From 1975 to 1977 the enemies clashed frequently along the border. In 1977 the Cambodians attacked Vietnam, which launched a retaliatory attack. On Christmas Day 1978, more than 150,000 Vietnamese invaded Cambodia. In only two weeks, they overthrew the Khmer government and began 10 years of Vietnamese rule.

▼ These government troops in Cambodia were defeated by the Khmer Rouge in 1975.

1979, but soon left once they thought their displeasure had been made clear. The Vietnamese remained in control in Phnom Penh for some 20 years.

Communism in Laos

In Laos, civil war had broken out in 1964 among rightists, neutralists, and the Communist Pathet Lao. The fighting in Vietnam had further destabilized the country.

► A Cambodian visits the site of one of the killing fields, marked by a huge pile of skulls and bones.

KEY MOMENT

The Killing Fields

The name killing fields was coined by the Cambodian journalist Dith Pran to describe the mass graves where the Khmer Rouge buried large numbers of Cambodians. Between 1.7 and 2.5 million people died under Khmer rule from 1975 to 1979, of a total population of around 8 million. They were executed, or died of disease or starvation, as the Khmer drove the population from the cities to try to create a rural, farming society. So-called intellectuals and professionals were executed, along with non-Khmer ethnic groups, Buddhist monks, and Christians and Muslims.

The North Vietnamese wanted to protect the Ho Chi Minh Trail in Laos, the route by which they moved supplies to the South. The Americans carried out a secret bombing campaign, while the CIA armed anti-Communist guerrillas in Laos. In 1971 the United States backed a South Vietnamese invasion of Laos that was repulsed by the North Vietnamese Army.

In February 1973, a month after the end of the Vietnam War, the Vientiane Agreement created a new coalition government. But when South Vietnam and Cambodia fell to the Communists in 1975, the Pathet Lao seized power. The 600-year-old monarchy came to an end, and Prince Souphanouvong became head of the new state of the Lao People's Democratic Republic.

Vietnam's future

For their part, the Chinese had begun to mend relations with the West, while Vietnam remained an international pariah. After the invasion of Cambodia, Vietnam was disqualified from most international aid and remained one of the poorest countries in the world. Inflation reached 600 percent, and Vietnam could not grow enough food to feed its people. Famine became a regular occurence as agricultural productivity fell but the birth rate reached 3 percent, one of the highest rates in the world.

In the 1980s Vietnam's Communist rulers introduced "renovation," which allowed some elements of the market economy to return.

They entered discussions with the United States about the fate of American personnel missing in action (MIAs). They also withdrew from Cambodia in 1988. In 1991,as the Cold War came to an end, the Soviet Union cut all aid to Vietnam. That speeded up the growth of the market economy and the return to normal relations with the United States, which was completed by 1994. Nearly 30 years after the ground war had begun in earnest, the two enemies were reconciled.

▼ Mao Zedong (left) meets U.S. Secretary of State Henry Kissinger in November 1973, as part of the improved relations between China and the United States.

GLOSSARY

boat people Refugees who fled Vietnam by sea after the Communists came to power in 1975.

coalition A group of countries acting together to achieve a particular goal of benefit to all of them.

collectivize To create communities in which property is owned by a community rather than by individuals.

diplomatic Relating to the peaceful relations between governments.

doctrine A statement of official government foreign policy.

federation A league formed by amalgamating states into a group.

guerrilla Someone who fights by irregular means such as ambush, sabotage, and assassination.

hardware The physical means by which to wage war, including weapons, vehicles, ships, and aircraft.

ideological Related to a system of political beliefs, such as Communism.

Indochina A peninsula in Southeast Asia that includes Myanmar, Cambodia, Laos, Thailand, and Vietnam; also the French colony that formerly occupied much of the region.

intelligence Any information gathered about the enemy, particularly by reconaissance or espionage.

nationalism The desire of a people to govern themselves in their own country.

nonaligned Not in an alliance with any other country or power bloc.

protocol A code of correct conduct.

Parallel One of a series of evenly spaced imaginary lines that circle the Earth in an east–west direction.

telex A communications system with teletypewriters joined by a telephonic network.

Viet Cong A guerrilla member of the Vietnamese Communist movement.

Vietminh The Vietnamese Communist movement in the 1940s.

FURTHER RESOURCES

Books

Gitlin, Marty. *U.S. Involvement in Vietnam* (Essential Events). Abdo Publishing Company, 2010.

Gunderson, Megan M. *Lyndon B. Johnson: 36th President of the United States* (United States Presidents). Abdo Publishing Company, 2009.

Johnson, Kristin F. *Ho Chi Minh: North Vietnamese President* (Essential Lives). Abdo Publishing Company, 2011.

Kent, Deborah. *The Vietnam War: From Da Nang to Saigon* (The United States at War). Enslow Publishing Inc, 2011.

McNeese, Tim. *The Cold War and Postwar America, 1946–1963*. Chelsea House Publications, 2010.

O'Connell, Kim A. *Primary Source Accounts of the Vietnam War* (America's Wars through Primary Sources). Myreportlinks.com, 2006.

Tougas, Shelley. *Weapons, Gear, and Uniforms of the Vietnam War* (Edge Books). Capstone Press, 2012.

The Vietnam War (Perspectives on Modern World History). Greenhaven Press, 2011.

Wiest, Andrew. *The Vietnam War* (Essential Histories: War and Conflict in Modern Times). Rosen Publishing Group, 2008.

Websites

http://www.pbs.org/wgbh/amex/vietnam/
Online companion to the PBS series *Vietnam: A Television History*.

www.history.com/topics/vietnam-war
History.com page of links about the Vietnam War.

http://www.spartacus.schoolnet.co.uk/vietnam.htm
Spartacus Educational page with links to biographies and other articles.

INDEX